food processing

ANNE BARNETT

D1081323

1507585

Heinemann
LIBRARY

H www.heinemann.co.uk/library
Visit our website to find out more information about Heinemann Library books.

To order:
☎ Phone 44 (0) 1865 888066
▤ Send a fax to 44 (0) 1865 314091
▢ Visit the Heinemann Bookshop at www.heinemann.co.uk/library to browse our catalogue and order online.

First published in Great Britain by Heinemann Library,
Halley Court, Jordan Hill, Oxford OX2 8EJ,
a division of Reed Educational and Professional Publishing Ltd.
Heinemann is a registered trademark of Reed Educational & Professional Publishing Limited.

OXFORD MELBOURNE AUCKLAND
JOHANNESBURG BLANTYRE GABORONE
IBADAN PORTSMOUTH NH (USA) CHICAGO

© Reed Educational and Professional Publishing Ltd 2003
The moral right of the proprietor has been asserted.

Designed by AMR
Illustrations by David Woodroffe
Originated by Ambassador Litho Ltd
Printed by Wing King Tong

J664
1507585

ISBN 0 431 14042 1 (hardback)
07 06 05 04 03
10 9 8 7 6 5 4 3 2

ISBN 0 431 14049 9 (paperback)
07 06 05 04 03
10 9 8 7 6 5 4 3 2 1

British Library Cataloguing in Publication Data
Barnett, Anne
  Food processing. – (Trends in food technology)
  1.Food industry and trade
  I.Title
  664'.02

Acknowledgements
The Publishers would like to thank the following for permission to reproduce photographs:
Air Products: p36, 37; Anthony Blake Photo Library: p13, 19, Maximilian Stock pp7, 17, Rosenfeld Image p18, Joy Skipper p35; Atlantic Syndication: p24; Chris Honeywell: p16; Corbis: p41; Gareth Boden: pp5, 11, 12, 14, 21, 26, 27, 29, 30, 32, 33, 43; Science Photo Library: p34; Stock Market: p39; Tudor Photography: pp4, 22, 25, 31

Our thanks to Alison Winson for her comments in the preparation of this book. The author thanks the following people: Clare Barnett-Thomas, Toby Barnett, Roy Ballam, Claudia Leyen and her daughter, Anouska, Clive Beecham, David Hume and the employees of Kinnerton confectionery, Terry Chapman, Linda Young and members of The Department of Health and the Food Standards Agency.

Cover photograph reproduced with permission of Stock Market.

Every effort has been made to contact copyright holders of any material reproduced in this book. Any omissions will be rectified in subsequent printings if notice is given to the Publisher.

Any words appearing in the text in bold, **like this**, are explained in the glossary.

contents

what is food processing?

The raw materials from which food is produced come from three sources. These are:
- animals
- plants (including **fungi**)
- fish.

These raw materials are called commodities, as they can be bought and sold for profit. They are essential to the food industry because it is from these raw materials that more complex products are made.

Processing is what is done to raw materials to turn them into products we can eat. Almost all the food we eat has been processed in one way or another. Imagine how we would feel about eating potatoes which were cooked without first being cleaned? The term **conversion** is also used to describe processes in food technology.

▼ *These carrots are being prepared using primary processing methods — in this case, chopping.*

Primary processing

There are two types of processing. One is called primary processing. This is when raw materials (called **primary products**) are treated to make them edible. The simplest methods of this process include washing, peeling, chopping, ageing and butchery (hanging and cutting up of meat). There is also squeezing, shelling and gutting (of fish). More complex processes such as the milling of wheat to make flour and the production of sugar are also examples of primary processing.

Secondary processing

The other type of processing is called secondary processing. This is the conversion of primary products into edible food products. A good example of secondary processing is the conversion of flour into various products, including pasta and different types of bread. Other examples of secondary processing are the conversion of milk to butter and cheese; also the production of all ready-to-eat convenience products.

Through secondary processing flour can be turned into other products, such as bread or pasta. ▶

The effect of processing

Processing can change the flavour, colour, texture, appearance, aroma and nutritional value of food. The changes that take place depend on the physical and chemical characteristics and properties of the food. Some processes create a temporary change, that is one that can be reversed, for example, melted chocolate will become solid again on cooling. The effect of most processes however is to make a permanent change, that is one which cannot be reversed. For example, butter, flour, sugar and eggs are permanently changed when combined to make a cake.

Everyone involved in food processing and designing food products must have a knowledge of basic food science in order to understand the effect of a process on food ingredients or primary food products.

Secondary procedures

One or a combination of the following procedures may be used to produce a specific product:

- mixing — the ingredients are mixed together to form the consistency required for the product
- depositing/forming/moulding — a predetermined amount of the mixture is put into a container or it is moulded/formed into the desired shape
- **enrobing**/covering — a product may be covered with a coating, such as icing on a bun
- layering/dividing — parts of the mixture are placed on top of each other to produce layers of different textures, for example in Kit Kat® chocolate biscuits, or the product is divided into smaller parts, as when Kit Kat® is sectioned into two or four 'lines'
- extruding — the ingredients are pushed through a metal disc, called a die, to make a specific shape, as in mincing and the shaping of spaghetti
- drying — moisture may be removed in order to lengthen the product's shelf-life
- fortifying — other ingredients may be added to improve various aspects of the product; either for nutritional fortification (for example margarine is fortified with vitamin D) or to improve the **functional properties** of ingredients, as when a stabilizer is added to mayonnaise ingredients
- aerating — a process that lightens mixtures to make them more palatable; various methods are used including the addition of a raising agent, or whisking and beating a mixture to incorporate air
- heating/cooking/cooling — the final procedures used to produce an end product.

food processes

Small-scale food processing takes place in the domestic kitchen. On a larger scale, food is processed in factories and bakeries. Whether food is produced as individual products or scaled-up to produce large numbers of one product, the processes used are the same. These processes are referred to as **unit operations**. They are carried out in sequence. The flow chart below shows the unit operations and the sequence in which they take place.

Storage, sorting and preparation
of raw materials
↓
Mixing
↓
Depositing and forming
↓
Cooking and cooling
↓
Filling and coating
↓
Packaging and storage

Storage, sorting and preparation

Storage — The raw materials must be handled hygienically and stored appropriately. Perishable foods in chilled storage must be kept at a temperature slightly below 8°C to reduce spoilage by **enzymes** and **micro-organisms**. Food that is to be frozen must be frozen quickly and kept at a temperature of about −18°C.

Sorting — Food is separated into groups by size, colour or weight. It is also graded according to its quality, for example, the degree to which it is free from contamination and damage.

Preparation — Sometimes the food has to be trimmed, by cutting, slicing, grinding, shredding, pulping or crushing, to make it the right size, shape and/or texture for further processing. Ingredients must also be formulated according to what is being produced. This involves weighing and measuring ingredients to ensure that the amounts of each and the proportion of one ingredient to another are accurate.

Mixing

This stage involves the mixing or dispersion of solids and liquids or gases or any combination of these. The method of mixing varies according to the ingredients and the type of end product required. For example, the mixing mechanism required to process a soft biscuit dough must be slow and gentle in order to disperse the ingredients, so the dough is slowly folded over and over itself. This gives a soft, 'melt in the mouth' texture to the finished product. By contrast, a hard dough must undergo a kneading action, which is much harsher and more powerful.

Liquids are easier to mix than solids, but **immiscible** liquids must be **emulsified**. High-speed propellers are sometimes used to mix liquids; tumbler mixers are used for dry powders; and 'Z' blades for **viscous** mixtures.

Depositing and forming

A continuous process is used in most cases so that large amounts of the

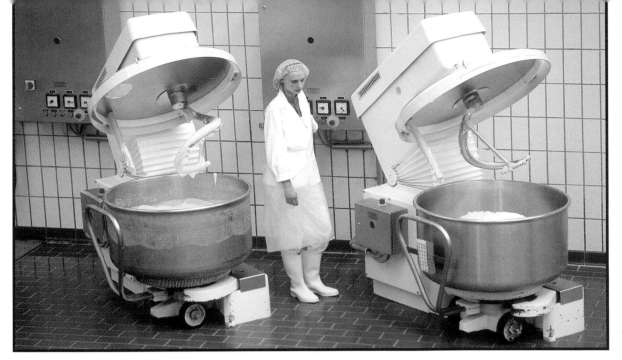

▲ *These machines use a powerful kneading action to produce a hard dough.*

product can be made. The product should also be of consistent quality. For example, a measured amount of cake mixture is deposited into tins, and products such as swiss rolls are first made into sheets and then cut and rolled to specific sizes and shapes.

Cooking and cooling

In most instances products are moved through an oven on a steel conveyor belt. The temperature and timing of cooking vary according to the type of product. In some smaller factories, products are baked in a set of large ovens, and each may be set at a different temperature according to the needs of the product. There are always four steps in the process:

1 development — the mixture begins to change from raw to the cooked state
2 setting — the shape becomes distinct
3 drying — the mixture becomes set in its final textural state
4 colouring — the required degree of browning takes place.

Filling and coating

After baking, products are finished in a variety of ways, such as filling and coating. For example:
- sponge cakes are filled with jam and/or cream
- filled fruit pies may be dusted with icing sugar
- biscuits may be **enrobed** with icing or chocolate.

Packaging and storing

When products are packed for storage and distribution, various checks take place. These include check-weighing which ensures that the product is the right weight, and metal detection which ensures that there are no metal objects in the finished product.

Packaging protects the product and helps to prolong its life. It can also carry information for the consumer, such as nutritional content. The packaging may also enhance the appeal of the product and encourage the consumer to buy it.

fats and oils

In order to make a product successful, it is important to understand something about the structure of the ingredients used in food processing. The properties and characteristics of ingredients can be changed by heating, removing heat, and combining them with other ingredients. The next section explains the properties of the different food groups used in food processing.

Lipids

The words 'fats' and 'oils' do not refer to different substances, they refer to the physical appearance (state) of the same type of substance. Put simply, fats are solid and oils are liquid. For example, fats such as butter and margarine are solid at room temperature; in contrast, oils such as olive oil are liquid at room temperature. The overall term which describes both fats and oils is lipids.

Lipids are made up of triglycerides. A triglyceride consists of fatty acids containing carbon, hydrogen and oxygen, which are mixed with an alcohol component called glycerol. A molecule of glycerol has three groups of combined hydrogen and oxygen called **hydroxyl** groups. When each of the three hydroxyl groups has combined with a fatty acid, a triglyceride is produced.

Types of lipids

When all the carbon in a lipid is attached to hydrogen the fatty acids are said to be saturated. When some of the carbon is not attached to hydrogen the fatty acids are said to be unsaturated.

The more saturated fatty acids that are present, the harder the state of the lipid. The more unsaturated fatty acids that are present, the softer the state of the lipid, as in soft margarine.

What do lipids do?

Knowing about the **functional properties** of lipids is useful in cooking.

Shortening — Fats can shorten mixtures. This means that when fat (such as lard or margarine) is combined with other ingredients to make pastries or biscuits, the end result is 'crumbly' (short). Ordinarily, **gluten**, a strong stretchy substance, is produced when flour and water are mixed. When gluten is allowed to develop in a mixture, it creates a strong, elastic dough which would make some pastries and biscuits tough. The introduction of fat, however, coats the flour, preventing the absorption of a lot of water. As a result, gluten development is reduced. When fat coats the flour the dough remains soft with little 'stretch', and a short, crumbly texture results.

Smoothness — Fats can prevent lumps from occurring in sauces thickened with flour. The fat surrounds the flour particles so that when the flour is beaten with liquid, it does not swell up and 'clump', and a smooth sauce results.

Rising — Fats help mixtures to rise. Cakes and other products need to have air 'trapped' into the mixture to enable them to become light and rise. When fat is creamed with sugar, air is incorporated and held in the mixture. The air forms small bubbles and a **stable foam** is produced, which helps the mixture to rise when heat is applied since air expands when heated.

Plasticity — The property of fat that produces its mouldable and pliable effect is called plasticity. It enables fat to be spread in layers, as in the production of puff pastry. For this product, layers of flour dough are separated from each other by layers of fat by rolling and folding (see diagram). During cooking the fat layers are absorbed by the dough layers and the product rises as a result of the air, which has been trapped between the layers, expanding as well as the water in the dough evaporating to steam. The result is a 'flaky' puff pastry.

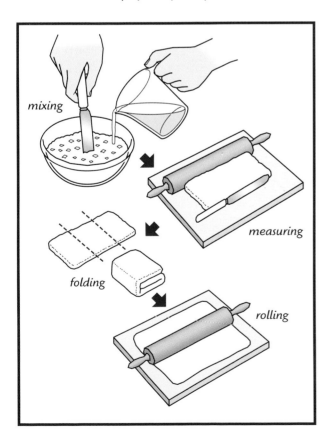

mixing

measuring

folding

rolling

Freshness — Some fats prevent moisture loss from baked products, which increases the length of time the product remains fresh and moist. Other fats are used to **baste** foods that are cooked in dry heat, such as grilling and roasting.

Non-stick — Greasing a cooking container with fat prevents food from sticking to it.

Sensory attributes — When fat is added to a sauce or put on top of cooked vegetables, a shine or gloss results. Fats can also provide colour, aroma and flavour. These **sensory attributes** vary according to the type of fat. Some have strong flavours and aromas; others are bland, for example, olive oil has a stronger flavour and aroma than sunflower oil. A particular fat is chosen to suit the product.

Smoke point — This is the temperature at which a fat begins to break down into a gas and a sediment; in other words it decomposes. A light blue smoke, an acrid smell and an unpleasant flavour result, all of which will spoil the product. Each fat has its own smoke point and must be chosen appropriately to match the cooking process. If a product is to be fried, a fat with a high smoke point must be used. Most vegetable oils, with the exception of olive oil, have a smoke point of around 232°C, which is high.

◀ *Several layers of fat are added whilst producing puff pastry to ensure that it has a flaky quality when cooked.*

proteins and carbohydrates

Proteins

The **functional properties** of proteins vary according to the shape and chemical nature of the protein. All proteins are made up of molecules of amino acids joined in a long chain. Amino acids are compounds containing carbon, hydrogen, oxygen and nitrogen. Each protein has its own number and sequence of amino acids. The shape of the protein molecule often determines its functional characteristics.

The protein structure of a substance can be altered in several ways:
- the application of heat
- mechanical action
- the addition of some salts
- a change of **pH**.

The process of change is called denaturation. When denaturation occurs the chains of amino acids that make up a protein unfold and the structure changes.

Egg protein

The protein structure of an egg can be changed in the following ways:

Heat — When an egg is boiled the egg protein coils unfold and a solid network is formed which sets the egg. This is called **coagulation** and it occurs at a temperature of between 60°C and 70°C.

Mechanical action — The denaturation of protein in eggs occurs when egg white is whisked and a **foam** is produced. This change is partially reversible in that if the uncooked foam is left for a while the egg white becomes liquid again, although it can never be whisked again to achieve the same degree of foam.

Salt and pH — When an egg has been stored for some time the pH rises, because carbon dioxide is lost during storage. An egg-white mixture with a high pH (more alkaline than acid) takes longer to produce a good foam, which means that the denaturation process is slowed down and a less perfect product is the result. The addition of cream of tartar (a salt) to an egg white speeds up the process because it is an acid-based substance, which lowers the pH.

Other proteins

Gliadin and glutenin — These are two proteins found in flour. When mixed with water they make an elastic stretchy substance called **gluten**. In bread dough, gluten forms a 3-D network which gives structure to the bread and helps to keep air and gases in the dough. The air and gases expand when heated and cause the dough to rise.

Gelatin — This protein is made from collagen, the connective tissue in meat. When mixed with warm water the protein molecules unwind. When cooled, they form a stable network that traps the liquid and sets the mixture. This is a reversible change since the set product will become liquid again when heated.

Carbohydrates

Many foods contain carbohydrates. They form a wide range of natural substances and include starches and sugars. Starch is

All these products will contain sugar as a flavouring.

the material in which plants store their energy. It exists as granules, which are shaped differently according to the plant source. Sugars are **soluble** in water and taste sweet.

Carbohydrates are grouped by size:
- monosaccharides ('mono' meaning one), e.g. glucose
- disaccharides (two monosaccharides), e.g. maltose
- polysaccharides (many monosaccharides), e.g. starch

They have various functional properties that are useful in food production.

Dextrinization — This occurs when bread is toasted, cakes are baked and meat is roasted or grilled. It is caused by a reaction between a sugar and protein contained in the food. The reaction forms brown-coloured compounds called dextrins. The brown compounds change the colour, aroma and flavour of the food. It is known as non-enzymic browning or the Maillard reaction (after the scientist who discovered the effect).

Gelatinization — When starch, for example in flour, is mixed with water and heated, the granules of starch soften, swell and absorb the liquid. At this stage the mixture changes from a thin and watery liquid to a thicker one. This is called gelatinization. The more starch in proportion to liquid there is, the thicker the mixture becomes. The thickness is

referred to as **viscosity**. When the mixture cools down it forms a gel. Blancmange is an example of a product set by gelatinization of starch.

Caramelization — When sugar is added to water it dissolves, and if the water is heated a syrup forms. During further heating, the water dissolves as vapour, the syrup thickens and changes from light to dark brown. This is a chemical change and is not reversible. The resulting substance is caramel which has a toffee-like flavour and is used to colour and flavour custards, ice cream and mousses.

Preservation — When a large proportion of sugar is used in a product it delays spoilage by inhibiting **micro-organism** growth, lengthening the shelf-life of a product. In the **formulation** of jam, for example, a high **concentration** of sugar is used in proportion to fruit.

Flavour development — Sugar, usually in the form of sucrose, is used to add flavour to a variety of products. Cakes, tomato sauce and biscuits are all examples. In savoury products, the sugar acts as a flavour enhancer. The flavours of the other ingredients mix well and seem stronger.

combining ingredients: solutions

In food processing it is useful to know what happens when certain types of food ingredients are mixed and when heat is applied or removed.

Solvents and solutes

A **solution** is a liquid (called a **solvent**) in which one ingredient or more has been dissolved. An ingredient that dissolves in a solvent is called a **solute**. For example:

- syrup is a solution of sugar (the solute) and water (the solvent)
- brine is a solution of salt (the solute) and water (the solvent)
- fizzy drinks are solutions of carbon dioxide gas (the solute) and water (the solvent).

Solutions can be:

- diluted — containing only a small amount of solute
- concentrated — containing a large proportion of solute to solvent
- saturated — containing so much solute in proportion to solvent that no more will dissolve.

Water molecules have positive and negative charges, which means that water is a polar solvent. Sucrose molecules also have a number of positive and negative charges. The negatively charged parts of sucrose are attracted to the positively charged parts of water molecules and vice versa. In a sugar solution the molecules in the sucrose crystals become separated and disperse to produce the solution.

Properties of solutions

The ingredients in a solution change their state during the mixing process. However, the changes which take place in many solutions are not permanent. For example, vinaigrette dressing is a solution of oil and vinegar, which when shaken together will mix, but when left to stand, will separate from each other.

If a solution is heated, more of the solute can be dissolved. For example, heated syrup forms the basis of a number of products, jam being the most well-

When left to stand, the oil and vinegar in a vinaigrette dressing will separate. ▶

During jam production, the fruit must be boiled with sugar and water.

known. The higher the temperature reached, the more sugar can be dissolved. Syrup boils at a higher temperature than the normal boiling point of water, which is 100°C. When syrup boils, the water gradually evaporates and the **concentration** of the solution increases. This raises the boiling point of the solution. The more sugar the solution contains, the higher the temperature at which it boils.

% Sugar	40	50	60	70	80	90
Boiling point (°C)	101.5	102.5	103.0	106.5	112.0	130.0

Getting the relationship between sugar content and boiling point right is essential in successful jam-making. The large proportion of sugar used to make jam lengthens the shelf-life of fruit as well as making a new product. The sugar delays the spoilage of fruit by inhibiting **micro-organism** growth. In the **formulation** of jam, a high proportion of sugar is used in proportion to fruit.

Successful jam cannot be made without the help of a carbohydrate called pectin. Although most fruits contain pectin, apples and blackcurrants contain the most. During jam production sugar, water and fruit are boiled together and pectin is released from the cell walls of the fruit. When the mixture cools the pectin produces a 'set' or gel. For gelling to occur the mixture must be fairly acidic, that is have a low **pH** (about 3.2). In the

commercial production of jam pectin and citric acid are added to make sure a good set is achieved.

How does pectin work?

During the boiling process in jam making, the pectin in the fruit becomes **soluble** and is dispersed throughout the mixture as a sol (see page 14). The acidity of the mixture and the sugar reduce the ability of pectin to attract water and as a result, on cooling, a network of pectin molecules is formed which holds a **viscous** sugar solution. The hydrated pectin molecules remain separate and do not form a firm gel. Very small amounts of pectin can hold large amounts of sugar in a gel. If there is insufficient pectin present a soft, runny jam is produced.

combining ingredients: colloids

A colloidal system is produced when one substance is distributed or dispersed in another without forming a **solution**. The substance which is dispersed (sometimes referred to as scattered) is called the disperse phase. The substance within which it is suspended is called the continuous phase. For example, in a **foam** made with egg white, the air bubbles, which are trapped in the egg white, are the disperse phase; the egg white itself is the continuous phase.

Types of colloidal system

The type of colloidal system is determined by the state of the two substances that are mixed together.

Sol — A liquid colloid is called a sol. An example of a sol is unset jelly. The gelatine is dissolved in water.

Gel — A solid colloid is called a gel. As the gelatine in water cools, the molecules of gelatine form a continuous network throughout the liquid and a gel is formed. This happens when jelly sets.

The use of a starch to set or thicken a liquid has the same effect — for example, when making blancmange. In this case,

there is an attraction between the starch and the liquid molecules, and a network of starch molecules is formed. When hot these form a sol, and when cooled they become a gel. Sols and gels are known as lyophilic ('liquid-loving') colloids.

The table below shows some examples of products and their colloidal systems.

▼ *When jelly sets, a gel is formed.*

Emulsions

Emulsions are a type of colloidal system. These can be liquid in liquid (oil in water) colloids as in mayonnaise, or

System type	Disperse phase	Continuous phase	Product example
Sol	Solid	Liquid	Jelly not yet set
Gel	Liquid	Solid	Set jelly, jam
Emulsion	Liquid	Liquid	Milk, mayonnaise
Solid emulsion	Liquid	Solid	Butter
Foam	Gas	Liquid	Whisked egg white, whipped cream
Solid foam	Gas	Solid	Cake, bread, ice cream

liquid and solid (water in oil — the oil being in a solid form) as in margarine. Mayonnaise is a colloid made by the suspension of droplets of oil in vinegar. To get the ingredients to mix in the first place, some mechanical force must be used, for example vigorous shaking or beating, because the two ingredients are **immiscible**. This type of emulsion is not **stable** and when left for a while the two substances will separate. In order to make successful mayonnaise, a stable emulsion must be produced. This is done by the addition of an emulsifying agent called an emulsifier. In mayonnaise, egg yolk is used along with the oil and vinegar because it contains an emulsifier called lecithin. The lecithin prevents the separation of the oil and vinegar.

How do emulsifiers work?

The water-**soluble** part (**hydroxyl**) of an emulsifier molecule is attracted to water, and the oil-soluble part (**stearate**) is attracted to oil.

▼ *A stable emulsion is produced with the use of an emulsifier.*

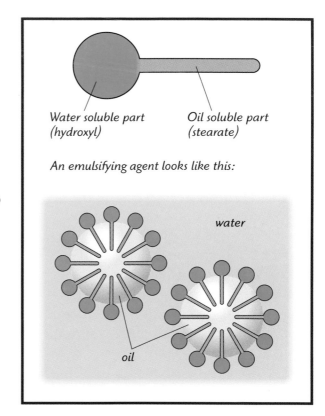

Water soluble part (hydroxyl)   Oil soluble part (stearate)

An emulsifying agent looks like this:

water

oil

The emulsifier prevents oil droplets from coming together (called coalescing) and forms a stable emulsion by preventing separation of the two phases.

Foams

Ice cream is a foam produced from a partially frozen continuous phase in which air cells are dispersed. It is an oil in water emulsion.
- Dairy ice cream must contain not less than 7.5 per cent milk-solids-not-fat (referred to as SNF in the industry) and not less than 5 per cent milk fat.
- Non-dairy ice cream is made with vegetable fat and skimmed milk.

To make ice cream, the ingredients are mixed, heated and then frozen rapidly to prevent the formation of large ice crystals, which would spoil the texture. The mixture is then stirred vigorously to incorporate air, which increases the volume. (This bit of the process is called 'overrun' in industry)

Hard ice cream has an overrun of 100 per cent. This means that the basic mixture doubles its volume during mixing. Soft ice cream has an overrun of 50 per cent (this is because less air is beaten in).

combining equipment

Combining food is not only about ingredients – the equipment and processes that are used to mix the ingredients are also important. They must be appropriate for the product being made.

Industrial equipment

The equipment used for large-scale food production is much the same as domestic equipment, but because the amount and volume of ingredients are bigger, larger pieces of equipment are also required. Mechanically operated equipment is used for some processes in order to achieve consistent quality more speedily. Mechanical equipment also saves money and labour when a large amount of the same product is being made.

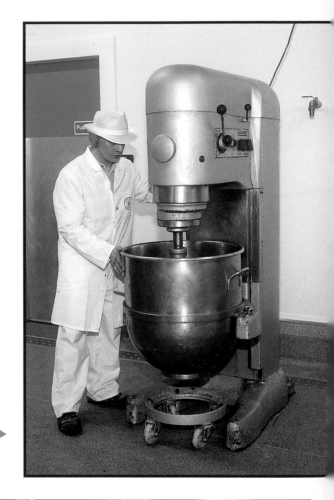

Industrial equipment is larger than domestic equipment which helps to ensure that the product is consistent. ▶

Equipment used	Reasons for use
Scales	To achieve exact amounts and proportions according to the **formulation**
Jugs etc. for the fluids	To achieve exact volumes according to the formulation
Sieves	To remove lumps, to ensure even distribution of dry ingredients
Graters, knives, food processor, cutters	To achieve particular shapes and sizes
Rolling pin, rollers	To achieve a specific thickness
Spoons, whisks, mixers, liquidizers, processors	To achieve particular consistencies
Piping bag, dies for **extrusion**	To control and shape a mixture which can be extruded

Here are some examples of the mechanical processes:

Rotary moulding — A number of stages are involved. First, pre-mixed ingredients, such as those used for burgers, are put into the hopper. The mix is then forced down the hopper onto an engraved roller that presses the required amount of mix into a mould.

Sheeting and forming — These processes ensure that the products are a uniform shape and size. Sheeting means rolling the mixture to make it flat; forming means cutting or moulding it to the desired shape. Dough, for example, may first need to be rolled into a continuous strip. Gauge rollers regulate the thickness of the dough, which then passes along a conveyer belt to be cut to shape. There may also be a design on the cutter which **embosses** the product.

Extrusion — Pre-mixed ingredients are placed in a hopper and pumped through a die (metal disc), which shapes the product into a continuous strip. The strip is then cut into uniform shapes which are carried away on a conveyer belt. Pasta shapes and some savoury snacks are made in this way.

Enrobing — Fish fingers and chocolate digestive biscuits are examples of **enrobed** products. In this process, the products are:
- moved along a conveyer belt
- (if necessary) dipped into or sprayed with a liquid to which a coating will stick (e.g. breadcrumbs on fish fingers)
- covered with coating (e.g. breadcrumbs for fish fingers; liquid chocolate for chocolate digestive biscuits)
- air-dried or vibrated to remove excess coating.

Fish fingers are examples of enrobed products.

heating equipment

Ovens

Commercial food processing usually requires large-scale heating equipment. The following oven types are often used:

Multi-deck ovens — These have several containers or chambers. The heat in each chamber can be individually controlled, which allows different products to be baked. These ovens are used in small-scale bakeries and some in-store bakeries.

Travelling ovens — These are large conveyor belt or tunnel type ovens. They can be several hundred metres long. The food travels along a belt through heated oven chambers.

Reel ovens — These have baking trays that revolve around a central point of heat to ensure even baking.

Rotary-rack ovens — Baking trays of products are wheeled into the oven cavity and attached to the roof so that they can be turned and rotated for even baking. Hot air is transferred by **convection** currents forced through vents in the walls of the chamber and passed over the products.

Heat exchange

During food processing, heat can be both applied or removed, according to the needs of the product being made. Heat is applied to make food
• safe to eat
• have good texture, taste and appearance
• digestible
• keep longer in good condition.

Heat is removed to:
• chill or freeze products
• increase keeping qualities and prevent spoilage
• alter the texture and appearance.

▼ *Industrial size ovens are used to cook large quantities of product at the same time.*

Microwave ovens can heat certain foods far quicker than a conventional oven.

Heat exchange works in the same three ways whether it is applied on a large industrial scale or a smaller domestic scale:

1 Convection currents — as in boiling and steaming, roasting and baking, blast freezing. The food must be in direct contact with a liquid or gas current.

2 Conduction — where the heat passes from a 'hot' object to a colder one. Dry frying is an example, where the heat from the hot pan is transferred to the food. The food must be in direct contact with the heat source.

3 Radiation — where the heat is transferred by rays. The rays move through the air until they come in contact with the food, when the heat energy they contain is transferred to the food.

A jacket potato is cooked by a combination of the first two methods. The initial application of heat is by convection to the outside surface which becomes hot. This heat is then conducted through to the centre of the potato. Grilled food is an example of the radiation method.

In some methods of cooking, the food is heated by another heated substance:
• boiling — the food is immersed in boiling water
• steaming — the food is surrounded by water vapour (steam)
• frying — the food is placed in hot fat.

How do microwaves work?

Microwaves are a type of electromagnetic radiation. They are a high energy source with short wavelengths. The short wavelengths mean that the waves reach a limited depth of the food being heated. The remaining mass is heated by the conduction of heat from the food which the microwaves have reached.

The waves will heat anything which contains water or moisture. They work by making the water molecules in the food oscillate (vibrate), which produces friction and consequently heat. The heat is then transferred across a 400mm depth of the food.

varying ingredients

Ingredients can be varied in a **formulation** in a number of different ways. Examples include the combination of different ingredients or the use of similar ingredients in differing proportions. However, when the ingredients are varied or combined a huge variety of products can be made. Take the following particular types of pastries as examples:

Short-crust pastry

Short-crust pastry is often used for covering fruit pies. The consumer expects the finished pastry to be short, 'melt in the mouth' and also crisp. These qualities can be achieved by:

- using half the amount of fat to flour
- mixing two types of fat (margarine or butter and a lard-type fat) — the margarine or butter gives a crisp quality and the lard-type fat makes the pastry short and 'melt in the mouth'
- using soft, plain flour with a low protein content. The protein in flour makes an elastic and stretchy substance called **gluten** when mixed with water, so the use of flour with a low protein content prevents the production of too much gluten, which would make the pastry tough
- adding a minimum of water — just enough that the dough can be rolled into shape, again preventing a tough texture.

Flaky-type pastries

Examples of these include puff pastry and flaky pastries. The consumer expects these pastries to be crisp and flaky (layered). Suitable qualities for flaky pastry can be achieved by:

- using $\frac{2}{3}$ to $\frac{3}{4}$ the amount of fat to flour (a greater proportion of fat)
- mixing two types of fat (as for short-crust pastry)
- using a strong flour with a high protein content, to make a glutenous, 'elastic' dough
- using a larger proportion of water to mix the dough in order to develop the gluten and make a 'stretchable' dough which can be rolled a great deal
- by rolling and folding the dough and fat to produce a number of layers of dough and fat (about four rollings).

The consumer expects puff pastry to be even richer, crisper, more flaky and layered than the flaky pastries above. These qualities can be achieved by:

- using all butter, which gives the required richness
- using the same amount of fat to flour (that is equal amounts of each)
- using strong flour (as for flaky pastry above)
- making a stretchable, elastic dough
- rolling and folding layers of fat and dough (about six rollings), cooling and resting the dough in between each rolling to make sure the fat does not melt.

Choux pastry

Consumers expect this pastry to be crisp on the outside and have a dry hollow inside. These qualities can be achieved by:

- making a thick sauce, called a panada, using 75 grams of strong flour and 125 millilitres of water to every two

The basic ingredients for most pastries are flour, fat and water. However, different textures and appearance can be achieved with the same ingredients by changing the proportion of one ingredient to another, using a particular type of an ingredient, and/or adding other ingredients, for example eggs. The way they are combined will also alter the end product.

eggs used. The large amount of water helps to make the products rise because it produces steam when heated, causing the pastry to puff up and become crisp

- adding the beaten egg gradually to the dough, to produce a consistency that is not too runny for **extrusion** through a piping tube. The dough is extruded into round or finger-type shapes, small enough to become crisp on the outside and dry inside when cooked.

Industrial production of pastry products

The ingredients in the formulations for large-scale production have to be increased in order to produce a large number of products. However, the quality of the finished pastry must meet consumers' expectations, so it is important for the manufacturer to make sure that the proportions of ingredients are accurate. The retailer tells the manufacturer what it wants the product to be like, by providing a **specification** for the product. This includes what its retail cost should be and how it should be packaged. The manufacturer needs to ensure these specifications are successfully met.

consistent products

Manufacturers aim to supply products that will be popular with the consumer and that will remain popular over a long period of time. The consumer making repeat purchases of the same product expects that the product will always be exactly the same standard on every occasion.

The consumer expects a consistent product always to be:
- of the same texture, size, weight, ingredient mix and ratio, value for money, taste and appearance
- safe to eat
- of a certain quality
- as described or advertised
- the same as the original **specification** used for its development.

Consumers do not like changes to be made to staple and favourite brands of products. A manufacturer who makes changes to these products may experience a drop in sales as consumers decide to buy a competitor's product instead.

How do manufacturers make sure products are of consistent quality?

The specification for the product will be very detailed and have built in tolerances and qualities which must be followed precisely.

Tolerances are part of the production process and indicate the slight variations in a process which are acceptable. An example is an ingredient weight of 100 grams. An acceptable tolerance would be 2 grams either side of 100 grams:

←98g	100g	102g →
beyond limits		*beyond limits*
action required		action required

In this example any weight below 98 grams and above 102 grams is beyond tolerance and would be rejected by the system. Action would be needed to rectify the system to make sure the correct weights are built in.

Consumers expect that their favourite products will be of a consistent standard every time they buy them. ▶

Anything which is out of tolerance in a system means that the product will not be consistent if production is allowed to continue.

Standard components

Standard components are vital in the making of food products, both on a domestic scale and in industry. Standard components are prepared ingredients that the manufacturer buys in from other manufacturers. They include such things as stock cubes, ready-made pastries, fruit-pie fillings and pizza bases. These components are designed and made by manufacturers to certain specifications which ensure that consistent products are always made. The use of standard components in any system saves time and effort, and ensures a high-quality outcome and high degree of consistency.

Baking powder is an example of a standard component. It is formulated especially to produce the required risen texture in some flour mixtures, such as that used to make Victoria Sandwich cakes. Baking powder is a mixture of sodium bicarbonate, an acidic substance, such as cream of tartar, and corn starch. These substances react when moist and produce the gas, carbon dioxide (CO_2). The CO_2 expands in heat, so when the cake **foam** is cooking, the gas is expanding at the same time, causing the cake to rise.

The amount of CO_2 given off indicates whether a baking powder is effective or not. Baking powder has a limited shelf-life, and if kept too long or in damp conditions the amount of CO_2 produced may be reduced.

Baking powder can be tested for effectiveness or compared with that made by a different manufacturer using the following test:
- make an egg white solution by mixing one tablespoon of egg white with one tablespoon of water
- measure out one 5ml spoon of baking powder
- mix the 5ml spoon of baking powder with the egg white solution in a 100ml cylinder
- heat gently, by putting the cylinder in a basin of hand-hot water and leave for a few minutes
- observe and measure the foam rising. If the foam does not rise after a few minutes, the powder will not be effective if used in a cake mixture and it should be thrown away.

Consistent products

The packaging of a product also contributes to the consistent quality of some products. For example, some cakes require special packaging to make sure they reach the consumer in peak condition. In this case the packaging helps to provide a consistent product. For example, the cakes are first wrapped in cellophane and then put into a box. The cellophane controls the transfer of water vapour from the cake, so it is kept moist and doesn't become stale. The box provides a rigid framework, reducing the risk of damage to the cake.

Domestic-scale recipes can be scaled up and ingredients combined to produce a product which fills a gap in the market. This case study concerns a specific product — a chocolate fudge cake — that was developed recently.

The gap in the market was related to allergy-safe food products. Allergies, in one form or another, are said to affect at least 40 per cent of the population at some point in their lives. For around two per cent of the population these allergies are potentially fatal. There is a condition where the body's immune system severely overreacts to something it recognizes as a foreign body. This is known as anaphylaxis. Such an acute allergic reaction needs immediate medical attention. The foods which most commonly trigger this type of reaction are peanuts, tree nuts (such as almonds, brazils, hazelnuts, cashews and walnuts), sesame seeds, fish, shellfish, eggs and dairy products.

Claudia's story

Claudia Leyens' daughter Anouska suffers from severe food allergies — in particular an allergy to nuts. Claudia knew that other ingredients, such as eggs and **gluten** in flour, created allergies in some people, so she decided to develop a cake which people who had these allergies could eat.

The difficulties that Claudia experienced when trying to find food that Anouska could eat, particularly fun foods such as birthday cakes, made her realize that the only way to have safe food was to create it herself.

▼ *Claudia Leyens with daughter Anouska, working on her allergy-safe chocolate cake.*

'I was determined to create a cake that was totally safe for virtually everyone and tasted wonderful too. I consulted a microbiologist and a professional cake maker who both told me it was impossible to make a cake without any egg that wouldn't turn out stodgy and flat. But I was determined to come up with a recipe that worked. I talked to my daughter's immunologist, Dr Gideon Lack of London's St Mary's Hospital, who was terribly encouraging but nevertheless thought it was a huge challenge. Then a friend gave me an old recipe her grandmother used to use. I played around with it, making my own adaptations, and finally without using any egg substitutes, I managed to come up with a 'chemical free' cake that worked.

'I spent all my free time baking, perfecting the recipe, so that it not only looked good but it tasted good too. I handed it out at my childen's nursery and to all my friends and family to taste and after six months I came up with a recipe for a moist rich chocolate cake which was totally safe.

'The next hurdle to overcome was actually getting someone to produce the cake. The reason so many foods found in supermarkets these days are labelled "not suitable for nut allergy sufferers" is due to the risk of **cross-contamination** during the manufacturing process.'

Eventually Claudia found a manufacturer who would take on her challenge.

The manufacturer's story

Kinnerton confectionery are chocolate manufacturers. They are the only company in the UK to have a totally nut-free zone in their factory. With an investment of £1 million, they created a mini-factory within their main factory, so that it is segregated into two distinct zones: 'nut' and 'nut-free'.

The managing director of Kinnerton, Clive Beecham, was keen to take on the challenge of producing the cake that Claudia had developed. From a commercial point of view, Clive Beecham was taking a large risk because the **duty of care** attached to such a product for this particular type of market exceeds the requirements for other products. For example, a simple **unit operation**, such as swabbing the surfaces, is a much lengthier and more expensive process than for other products. There are other expensive processes involved, particularly 'finishing' all of the cakes by hand. This is a very labour-intensive and expensive stage in the production. However, Clive Beecham was committed to the whole idea and made sure that he had a successful result.

When the development was completed and the cake was in production Claudia said: 'I am really thrilled to see my cake up there on the supermarket shelves alongside all the famous names.' The cake is nut-free, dairy-free, **soya**-free, egg-free and is not genetically modified.

Sometimes the ingredients normally used in a **formulation** are not suitable for all consumers. In these cases, alternative ingredients are used. The aim is usually to make the product containing an alternative ingredient as near to the original as possible.

Meat-free products

These products meet the needs of consumers who do not eat meat and/or those who wish to increase their consumption of vegetable-based products. The alternative ingredients are often referred to as meat alternatives or meat analogues.

Quorn™

Quorn™ is a totally meat -free product marketed by Marlow Foods Limited. The main ingredient of all Quorn™ products is a myco-protein, made from a member of the mushroom family. Myco-protein is grown using a natural **fermentation** process similar to the process used in yoghurt production.

The manufacturer claims that Quorn™ is lower in fat than an equivalent meat product, which could make it useful in a slimming regime.

A range of products

In October 2000, Marlow Foods Limited launched a new Quorn™ product called fajitas, which are traditional Mexican fare. They are based on tortillas (soft, pancake-like products) which can be filled with a variety of savoury fillings. The fajitas are filled with Quorn™ pieces that are coated in spices, peppers, onions, salsa and sour cream.

Other products in Marlow's range include burgers, mince, fillets, sausages and 'cold cuts'. Notice how all the products replicate those made with meat!

▼ *Quorn ready meals.*

Other meat-free alternatives

Textured Vegetable Protein (TVP) is another alternative to meat. It is made from bundles of **extruded soya** protein. It can be cut into specific shapes or minced and then flavoured in different ways to make an appetizing product.

Tempeh is another meat alternative made from a fermented mass of soya. It is solid and can be sliced and flavoured before cooking.

Tofu is also made from soya. It is semi-solid and absorbs flavours from other foods very readily.

A sweet alternative to fat

Sugar can also be used as an alternative ingredient. Mostly this occurs in what otherwise would be high fat products. Biscuits are a good example. The **functional properties** of sugar that make it a useful alternative ingredient are:

- It gives texture and '**mouth feel**' to products. This is because it is hydroscopic (attracted to water). The sugar acts as a humectant — that is, it absorbs a lot of moisture from the atmosphere. It helps to prolong the shelf-life of a product by keeping it moist for longer. Fat also does this, but when a low-fat sweet product is required, sugar can be used as an alternative ingredient

- It helps to make baked products tender. This is because the sugar takes up some of the water which would otherwise be absorbed by the protein in flour. The development of **gluten** is restricted and a more tender, softer crumb is produced

- It helps to make products light. Aeration occurs when sugar is creamed with fat, and air bubbles are formed within the mixture. These expand on heating, making the product rise and giving it a light texture. This action can be used when there is a need to reduce the amount of fat in a formulation.

A selection of meals made from meat–free alternatives.

additives

Additives are substances that are added to food to improve its quality. There are four main reasons for their use:

1 to make food safe and lengthen its shelf-life
2 to alter the texture of food
3 to give it colour
4 to enhance its taste.

Additives can be natural, nature-identical or artificial/synthetic (see page 30 for more details of these categories). Where additives come from and how they are made determine their categorization.

There is a huge number of additives in current use, subject to very strict, legal rules. For example, the 1990 Food Safety Act makes it illegal to add anything to food which is harmful to health.

E numbers are given to all permitted additives except flavourings, which do not currently have them. All foods made after 1 January 1986 must have the E number or the actual name of the additive on the ingredients list.

Reactions to additives

There is a concern amongst some consumers about possible unpleasant physical reactions to additives in foods. In reality there are probably more examples of unpleasant reactions to other ingredients, such as peanuts, wheat and milk. However, there are some people who are sensitive to certain additives, mainly colours and preservatives. The information given on food labels enables hypersensitive consumers to avoid such additives.

The functions of additives

1 To make food safe and lengthen its shelf-life — There are two types in this category: preservatives and antioxidants.

Preservatives prevent **micro-organism** growth which could cause food spoilage and food poisoning. In this way they allow food to stay fresh for longer and also make it safe to eat.

Antioxidants preserve the appearance and taste of food. For example, E300 (L-ascorbic acid, i.e. vitamin C) stops cut fruit, such as apples, from turning brown. They do this by preventing a substance in the apple combining with oxygen in the air, which would otherwise cause browning to occur. They also stop food which contains fat from becoming rancid and developing an 'off' taste. They do this by preventing fats and oils from combining with oxygen.

2 To alter the texture of food — **Emulsifiers** and stabilizers are substances that can affect the texture of food. They usually work together: emulsifiers help water and oil to mix together and stabilizers help them to stay mixed. E401 (sodium alginate) is an example of a stabilizing agent. It is used in packet cheesecake mixes, ice cream, barbeque sauce mixes and many other products.

Other texture-altering additives include 'thickeners'. These do what their name suggests. They act like flour, cornflour and other starches that are used for thickening. Modified starch is a popular thickener, as is E412 (guar gum), which is

Manufacturers are required to list any additives used in their food products. ▶

used in such products as packet soups, fruit drinks, milkshakes and ice cream.

There are also anti-caking agents, which prevent lumps forming in powdery ingredients and foods. For example, they are used in salt to make it free flowing. E504 (magnesium carbonate) is an anti-caking agent. It is used in icing sugar, table salt, butter and ice cream.

Raising agents make food rise. An example, would be E500 (sodium bicarbonate), which is mixed with an acid substance to make baking powder.

Gelling agents are used to make food set. E440 (pectin), used in the production of jams and jellies, is an example.

3 To give it colour — Colouring agents are used to intensify the natural colour of a food, to replace colour lost during processing and to make products which are naturally colourless more attractive, for example some soft drinks. They can be natural or artificial.

An example of natural colouring is E150 (caramel), which gives a brown colour to the food and also acts as a flavouring agent. Typical products in which it is used include packet cheesecake mix, tinned peas, mint jelly and sauce, and gravy granules. Another natural colour is E140 (chlorophyll), made from plants. Its green colour is used in fats, oils and canned green vegetables such as peas, which would normally lose their colour when preserved in a liquid.

Artificial colourings (those that are produced synthetically) include E102, a yellow colour called tartrazine. It is used in many products including some sweets, fizzy drinks, brown sauce, salad cream and cheese rind.

4 To enhance its taste — Some of these are natural ingredients in everyday use, such as sugar, herbs and salt. Others, such as saccharin and aspartame are artificial sweeteners that give a sweetness many times more intense than sugar. They are used in small amounts in diet foods and soft drinks. Another artificial sweetener used in sugar-free confectionary is Sorbitol. Its sweetness is a similar strength to sugar.

Some other additives in this group are referred to as flavour enhancers. They act by bringing out the flavour of another food without giving the food their own flavour. E621 (monosodium glutamate) is an example. It is used in a large number of savoury foods.

flavourings

Food flavourings are concentrated preparations used in very small quantities to give food odour and taste. Herbs and spices are traditional flavourings that are still used in modern food production, but in addition, the food industry uses a wide range of flavourings that have been developed more recently.

The composition of most flavourings is a complex mix of ingredients usually found in a **solvent** or 'carrier'. Starches, rusk, edible gums and salt are used as carriers for powdered flavourings, whilst tasteless and odourless solvents are normally used for liquid flavourings, such as essences, for example, vanilla essence.

Types of flavouring

Flavourings can be divided into the following three broad categories:

Natural — These can either be naturally occurring plant materials, for example herbs and spices, or products made from natural sources, for example by extraction and distillation, as in the production of lemon oil. Only a flavouring that consists of entirely natural ingredients may be labelled natural.

Nature-identical — These are chemically synthesized flavouring ingredients that are identical to naturally occurring flavouring substances. When used in similar **concentrations** as the natural product they have exactly the same qualities and functions. If a flavouring contains even one nature-identical ingredient it must be called nature-identical rather than natural.

Artificial flavourings — These substances are also synthesized chemically. They have not yet been identified in nature but are often similar to substances of natural origin. The presence of one or more artificial ingredients makes the whole flavouring artificial, and it must be labelled as such.

▼ *Natural flavourings used in a curry.*

Where does flavouring come from?

Most of the food we eat contains flavour that is naturally present or has been formed during cooking. For example, more than 400 known natural flavourings exist in strawberries, over 200 have been identified in honey and coffee contains over 300 flavouring components.

How much is consumed?

Consumption of nature-identical and artificial flavouring substances is about 5 grams per person per year. Most of the individual substances are consumed at a rate of one milligram per person per year. This compares with the average total consumption of around 45 grams per person per year of essential oils from natural sources, mainly orange, lemon, peppermint and spearmint.

40,000 tonnes is sometimes quoted as the total annual consumption of flavourings in the UK; of these, about 2500 tonnes are essential oils from natural sources and about 250 tonnes are nature-identical and artificial flavouring substances. The rest consists of natural fruit juices and concentrates, solvents and carriers.

Flavouring controls

The use of flavourings is covered not only by the Food Safety Act of 1990, it is further governed by the voluntary code of practice of the International Organisation of the Flavour Industry. This code stipulates that substances which occur naturally in the diet or are nature-identical may be used unless they are explicitly restricted or prohibited. Artificial flavourings must be examined for toxicity (poisonous effects) and used only if they have shown no hazard at the anticipated level of use.

If a food contains added flavouring there is a legal obligation to specify this on the ingredients list, no matter how small the quantity used. There are so many flavouring components it makes the use of E numbers for flavours impractical, so they are not identified by a code number on the ingredients list. The name of a food on the label is designed to prevent the consumer being misled as to its contents. For example, a yoghurt may be called 'strawberry' or 'strawberry flavoured' or have a picture of strawberries on the label only if its perceived flavour (that is the flavour which the consumer experiences) comes wholly or mainly from real strawberries. If it tastes of strawberries but the perceived flavour is not mainly derived from the fruit, it must be called 'strawberry flavour' yoghurt.

potato crisps – a case study

Potatoes are **primary products**. There are many varieties, some of which are available at the beginning of the potato season (June/July) whilst others are harvested later. The best methods of cooking and preparation for a type of potato depend on its texture. Some potatoes have firm, waxy flesh and keep their shape when cooked whilst others develop either a floury or a sticky texture when cooked.

Potatoes can be used to produce a large variety of secondary outcomes — that is dishes or individual products. Certain types of potato are best used for particular cooking methods. For example, Maris Piper potatoes are good for making chips, while King Edwards are better for baking or mashing.

Processed potatoes

Potatoes can be processed in many different ways. They can be dried or canned so they are available in convenient, labour-saving forms. The quality of potatoes preserved by these methods is altered to some extent, as their **organoleptical** characteristics are different from the fresh product.

Potatoes can also be manufactured into very popular products, such as crisps. The potato-crisp market is worth a great deal of money to manufacturers and food retailers because there is such a huge consumer demand for these products.

The success of Pringles®

Pringles® are an example of a snack product made from potatoes. They are a type of crisp first available in the USA in 1968 and were launched in the UK in 1991. The face on the can is of a moustached 'gentleman' from the 1890s, designed to make the product look 'established' and to give the consumer a feeling of cheerfulness.

▲ There are many different types and flavours of crisps.

Pringles® are made of the following ingredients:
- potato flakes — these make up the base material and help to give the snacks the typical potato flavour
- wheat starch — this has similar properties to the potato flakes; it is made **gluten**-free during the manufacturing process
- cottonseed oil — this provides flavour and makes the snacks pleasantly oily

- corn meal (made from maize) — this makes the texture crisp
- maltodextrin — this is a modified starch/sugar made from maize, which gives a slight sweet taste; it also helps the snacks to brown during cooking
- emulsifier — this is made from rapeseed and helps to stop the ingredients from separating out and spoiling the texture
- water — this evaporates and disappears during heating
- dextrose — this helps the browning process
- salt — this enhances the flavour of the product by making it stronger
- seasonings — these are a mixture of herbs and spices
- added colours — these make the product look more attractive
- potato starch — this helps provide the potato flavour
- disodium inosinate and disodium guanylate — these enhance the flavour of the product.

The way the flavouring is introduced to the surface of the snack is a secret process. However, it is clear that the seasonings are sprinkled on the top and made to 'stick' to the surface.

It is claimed by the manufacturer that there are fewer broken Pringles® than other crisps because of the packaging used. The packaging is made up of:
- a liner — this has a modified polyethylene layer, an aluminium foil layer and a paper layer, all of which are approved for food use and provide a protective barrier

- a tube — made from partly recycled cardboard, which gives the can its strength
- labels — made of coated paper
- two lids — an inner, 'peelable' lid made of foil, and a PET (polyethylene tetraphthalate) reclosable lid, made from low density polyethylene
- metal base — made from tin-free steel and put onto the can after the product has been added.

The manufacturer also claims that Pringles® are relatively 'kind' to the environment because the cans take up less space than bagged crisps and therefore reduce the amount of transportation necessary for delivery.

▼ *The tube-like packaging of Pringles helps to protect the crisps during transportation.*

People have been preserving food for centuries. The process was first used to store food when it was fresh, plentiful and in season for as long as possible, so that there was a supply of food during the winter months. Popular methods included drying, salting, smoking and **fermentation**. Sugar **solutions** were also used to preserve fruit.

More recent methods may make use of the same or similar ingredients, but technological developments within the industry have allowed more efficient and quicker methods of carrying out preservation processes. In addition, other methods of preservation, such as blast freezing, have been discovered.

The principles of preservation

Micro-organisms, which are present in the environment and in food, cause food to deteriorate and in some cases, make it unsafe to eat. They can alter the texture, aroma and flavour of food if conditions are appropriate for their growth and development. There are three main groups of micro-organisms that cause food spoilage: **bacteria**, **yeasts** and moulds. **Enzymes** that are present in some foods also cause food to deteriorate, for example the enzyme which causes fruit to go brown when it is cut and exposed to oxygen in the air (see page 28).

In order to limit food spoilage by yeasts and moulds and to prevent the growth of bacteria in food, the conditions that encourage the growth of micro-organisms must be understood. All micro-organisms need three basic conditions to live and grow. These are:
1 warmth
2 moisture
3 food.

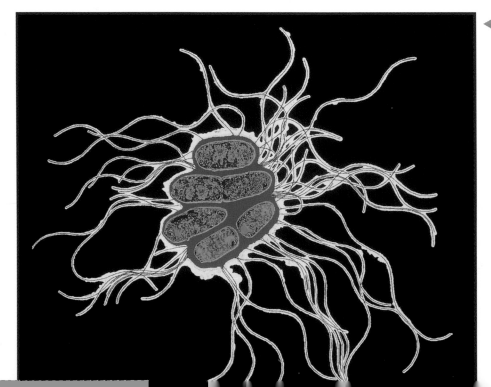

Salmonella bacteria can be responsible for certain types of food poisoning.

34

There are however, certain environments in which micro-organisms cannot live; examples include acidic solutions, such as vinegar solutions used in the pickling process, or a **concentrated** sugar medium, which reduces the amount of moisture available, as in jam-making. Preservation methods rely on the application of these facts.

Yeasts and moulds

These are always present in the air and are sometimes used beneficially in food production. For example, yeast is used as the raising agent in bread-making, and mould is introduced into 'blue' cheeses to give them their characteristic colour and flavour. However, both yeasts and moulds are also capable of spoiling food. Yeasts grow on sugary foods, causing fermentation. This is a production of bubbles of gas (carbon dioxide) and alcohol that changes the appearance and flavour of the food. Similarly, moulds grow a fuzzy 'hair' on the surface of food and make it unfit to eat.

When the conditions 'suit' bacteria they multiply and produce poisons, which are sometimes called toxins.

Toxic food poisoning

Some bacteria produce toxins when they are multiplying in food. If the toxins become separated from the bacterial cell they are called exotoxins. Exotoxins are poisonous. Heat destroys them, but in many cases a higher temperature is needed than it takes to destroy the bacteria from which they come. If food containing them is eaten, the toxins irritate the stomach and cause classic symptoms of food poisoning, such as vomiting, abdominal pain and diarrhoea.

Infective food poisoning

This is caused by living bacteria, which grow and multiply in the food. They have a substance inside the bacterial cell that is toxic. This toxin is called an endotoxin. This cannot be released from the bacterial cell until the bacteria die. If food contaminated with this type of bacteria is not heated sufficiently to kill the bacteria before it is eaten, food poisoning can result. The food must be heated sufficiently so that the endotoxins will also be destroyed.

preserving food: freezing

It is crucial to control the temperature of food according to the needs of the product. The application of heat, as in cooking, and the removal of heat, as in chilling and freezing, are both effective methods of making food palatable and safe to eat. (For information on the application of heat, see pages 38–39.) Both the application and removal of heat involve the transfer of heat to or from foods. This is called heat exchange and it is important in both domestic and industrial food production. The type of product required determines which method of heat exchange is used.

Removing heat from food is a way of preventing **enzyme** activity and destroying **micro-organisms**. The temperature required to do this varies. In the processes of chilling and freezing, the micro-organisms are not destroyed, but

their growth is slowed down. However, when the food is thawed and/or restored to normal atmospheric temperature the **bacteria** multiply at a faster rate, to make up for lost time.

Freezing methods

Plate freezing – The food is placed between refrigerated, hollow plates that exert slight pressure on the food, to remove air gaps. This system is used for large blocks of a product such as fish fingers before they are cut to shape.

Fluidized bed freezing – Jets of refrigerated air are blown up through the products, which float and remain separate. It is a continuous process used for products such as prawns, small pieces of vegetable and peas. The products are carried on a conveyer belt.

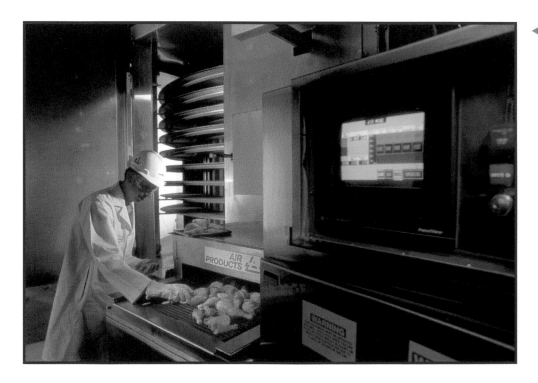

In blast freezing a strong fan is used to keep products, such as chicken, at a low temperature.

▶ Food, such as prawns, is sprayed with liquid nitrogen or carbon dioxide during cryogenic freezing.

Immersion freezing — Refrigerants (substances that are capable of cooling and freezing food on contact) are sprayed directly onto the food. This process is used to freeze fish at sea, directly after they have been caught.

Cryogenic freezing — This process is used for small products, such as prawns and soft fruit, as it ensures that the shape and texture of the products are not spoiled. The food is sprayed with liquid nitrogen or carbon dioxide, both of which create very low temperatures (liquid nitrogen −196°C and carbon dioxide −78°C). Carbon dioxide can be recycled within the system which makes it the more economical method.

Blast-freezing — This method uses powerful fans to circulate cold air, first over refrigerated elements and then over the food. The process brings about rapid cooling by reducing the insulating properties of the air on the surface of the food, which allows the food to be cooled quickly. Electrical devices called sensors measure the temperature and when it has reached the required level of cooling, further cooling is stopped and the temperature is held at that level.

Scraped heat exchangers — These are used when a smooth end product such as ice cream is required. The product is stirred and frozen at the same time. Rotating scrapers work against a cooled surface to prevent the formation of large ice crystals, ensuring a smooth consistency.

Disadvantages of freezing

Although freezing is a very successful method of preserving food, there are some disadvantages. It can alter the structure of some foods — for example strawberries become mushy and soft once thawed because the cell walls are damaged by the process; also some colloidal (thickening) systems separate and collapse.

Heating is an essential step in the cooking and preservation of food. At temperatures above 63°C and below 4°C, bacteria stop multiplying. This means that the range of temperatures in between marks the 'danger zone' that exists in all food production. Heating to temperatures above 63°C is therefore essential when cooking and preserving food.

Heat processing methods

Pasteurization

In this method, the food must be held at a temperature of at least 71.7°C for at least 15 seconds, followed by immediate cooling to around 3°C. The process increases the shelf-life of food by killing most of the **micro-organisms** which cause food spoilage and food poisoning.

The two main methods of industrial pasteurization are:

- batch pasteurization — The product is heated to a specific temperature, then held at that temperature for a specific period of time
- high temperature, short time (HTST) pasteurization — The product is heated to a high temperature for a short time, using a plate heat exchanger, and then cooled. Some fruit juices are preserved by this method.

Sterilization

This process lengthens the shelf-life of a product, provided it is not opened. In a batch process the products must be held at an approximate temperature of 115°C for about 20 minutes. This kills nearly all the micro-organisms in the food and prevents those which form spores from doing so. The products must be packed in an uncontaminated environment into air-tight containers.

The high temperature can cause the **organoleptic** characteristics of the product to alter. For example, sterilized milk has a slight taste of caramel.

Ultra Heat Treatment (UHT)

The legal requirement for this process (sometimes called Ultra High Temperature) is that the product must be held for at least one second at a temperature of not less than 135°C. The product moves continuously through the process which means that the texture, nutritional value, colour and flavour are retained to a greater extent than in the sterilization process.

Canning

In this process, the food is sterilized in air-tight containers. Micro-organisms and their spores are killed and because the product is sealed, re-contamination is prevented. Bottling is a similar process.

There are a number of stages to the canning process:

- Cleaning – All the raw materials are washed to remove possible contaminants.
- Sizing appropriately — Some ingredients, for example vegetables, have to be reduced in size or shape according to the product; they may be cut, sliced, minced or diced.
- Blanching — Vegetables must be blanched (immersed in boiling water) to prevent changes in colour and flavour that can be caused by **enzymes** in the untreated vegetables.

Cans on an assembly line being filled with a controlled amount of the product.

- Filling the cans — Fruits and vegetables are mixed with a **solution** such as a syrup or brine. Filling happens automatically. A measured amount of the product is deposited into the can, leaving a small space at the top to allow for expansion during heating.
- Sealing — Air is drawn out by a vacuum which seals the lid.
- Washing — This removes any food spilt on the outside of the can.
- Sterilization — The cans are put into a container called a retort, which works like a pressure cooker. Pressure ensures that the temperature reached is higher than the boiling point of water.
- Cooling — When the cans have been sterilized sufficiently they are cooled to prevent further cooking of the contents. Cool water is sprayed over them, causing the temperature and pressure to reduce gradually. If the cans were subject to a sudden drop in temperature and pressure, the seams of the can could be damaged and the product would become unsafe. The cans are put into a cooling tank to finish the process.
- Drying — Any water left on the surface of the can is left to evaporate to prevent rusting during storage.

- Labelling — A code that enables the product to be traced is stamped on the can and then labels are applied. Depending on the type of food inside some indication of shelf-life is included. This is indicated by a best before date on the label.

Irradiation

This process has similar preserving effects to pasteurization. It can be used to delay the ripening of fruit, kill micro-organisms and inhibit the sprouting of vegetables. The temperature of the food does not rise during this process so neither the taste nor the appearance is altered. However, there are some consumer concerns which focus on the safety of people involved in the process as well as the safety of those who consume irradiated food.

The fear that the food itself will be radioactive is unfounded. However, it is important that irradiated food is clearly labelled so that consumers have the choice of whether to buy it or avoid it. The food must be labelled either with the words, 'treated with ionizing radiation' or 'irradiated'.

Dehydration

This is when moisture is removed from food. **Micro-organisms** need moisture to live and multiply, they cannot grow without it. When moisture is removed from a product, its shelf life, safety and freshness are prolonged – it is preserved.

The process does not kill micro-organisms, but the product is safe because moisture has been removed.

The surface area of the food to be dried is sometimes increased by slicing and dicing the product which speeds up the rate of water loss.

Blanching is often carried out prior to drying to de-activate **enzymes** and prevent browning.

Dehydration methods

Sun drying – This is the oldest method of dehydration. It has been used for centuries and is practical only in hot climates. It is still in use for products such as sun-dried raisins and apricots.

Roller drying – The product is made into a paste or a liquid, then spread over heated drums or rollers that rotate. The heat evaporates all the moisture from the product, which is then scraped into a container. Products such as baby foods and 'instant' mash are dried in this way.

Fluid bed drying – This is used for small-sized products such as coffee and peas.

Fluid bed drying is a method used for small ▶ products, such as peas.

Warm air is blown from below the food particles or pieces and this dries them whilst keeping them separated.

Spray drying – Dried milk and coffee powder are dried in this way. A fine spray of the product in liquid form is introduced into a blast of hot air. This causes rapid evaporation of the liquid leaving behind a fine powder.

Accelerated freeze drying (AFD) – This produces the best quality dried products, but it is an expensive method. It is used for products which are at the luxury end of the market, such as some fruits and coffee. The product must first be frozen, then subjected to very high temperature in a vacuum, which changes the ice into water vapour without it first becoming

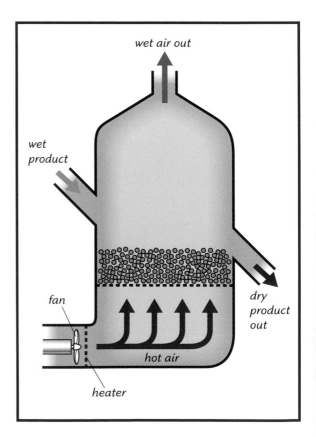

wet air out

wet product

fan

hot air

heater

dry product out

liquid — a process called sublimation. This method produces products which rehydrate (become liquid again) successfully. For example, the dried ingredients in instant cups of soup are very like fresh ones when water is added to the powder.

▲ *Racks of sprats being smoked to preserve their shelf-life.*

Alternative methods

Smoking — This is another method that has been used for centuries. Micro-organisms cannot live in a very smoky environment, so this method lengthens the shelf-life of the product. In addition, the flavour of the food is altered and a pleasant smoky aroma and taste develop. Chemicals are sometimes used in the process to speed up the time it takes and to help the product develop more flavour and colour. Examples of fish which are preserved in this way include herrings, which are called kippers in their smoked form.

Salting — Putting food in a brine **solution** or coating it with salt also lengthens its shelf-life. The salt reduces the moisture content of the food and therefore reduces the water available to micro-organisms, which need water to grow. The process naturally gives the product a salty taste, so it is not suitable for all foods.

Pickling — The food is covered with an acidic solution, such as vinegar. Micro-organisms prefer a neutral **pH**, so the acid prevents their growth. Onions can be preserved in this way and chutney is a pickled product.

Sugar solutions — When fruit is boiled in a sugar solution, as in jam-making, water is evaporated off until eventually there is none available for the micro-organisms and their growth is inhibited. In this way the fruit is preserved. Marmalades and jellies are also preserved in this way.

Fermentation — This is another ancient method. During **fermentation**, acids and alcohols are produced. These prevent the micro-organisms from gaining the moisture they require in order to thrive. Soy sauce is an example of a fermented product, as is **yeast**.

milk – a case study

Milk is an example of a **primary product**. It is made from the water and nutrients which the animals eat, so in this respect it could also be described as a **secondary product**. Cow's milk is the most popular type, but milk from other animals is also used.

Milk facts

- Milk is an **emulsion**, made up of droplets of fat suspended in a watery liquid.
- The carbohydrate that milk contains is a milk sugar called lactose.
- Milk has three proteins. The main one is casein; the others are lactalbumin and lactoglobulin.
- Calcium is the most important mineral present in milk. It also contains small quantities of zinc, magnesium and phosphorus.
- Milk contains the water-**soluble** vitamins riboflavin (vitamin B2), thiamin (vitamin B1) and nicotinic acid. The fat-soluble vitamins A and D are present in whole milk.

To preserve the quality of milk, most of it (99 per cent in the UK) is treated in one way or another.

The treatments

- *Pasteurized milk* – This is a heat treatment which makes the milk safe to drink and also extends its shelf-life. The milk goes through the HTST (high temperature, short time) process (see page 38). It naturally divides into layers, with fat in the form of cream floating on the top. Variations in fat content are available: whole (full-fat), semi-skimmed (which has some of the fat removed) and skimmed (majority of the fat removed).

- *Sterilized milk* – Unopened, this milk will keep for several months in an **ambient temperature**. There are no exact methods laid down for the sterilization procedure but legislation states that milk must be heated sufficiently to render it sterile (free of **micro-organisms**). During the processing the bottles are stacked into an autoclave (a strong sealed container) where steam, under pressure, raises the temperature to approximately 115°C for about 20 minutes. This causes a 'toffee-like' flavour to develop in the milk and some of the nutrients, particularly the B group vitamins, are destroyed. Whole, semi-skimmed and skimmed types are available.

- *Homogenization* – This treatment makes the fat droplets very small and evenly spaced in the milk so that it has a consistently smooth texture. The fat droplets are forced through a very small nozzle at high speed, which breaks up the droplets to about a quarter of their original size.

- *Ultra Heat Treated (UHT) milk* – This is sterilized homogenized milk. It is usually packed in heat-sealed cartons. While unopened it will keep for several months without refrigeration. However, once opened it must be treated as fresh milk, stored in the refrigerator and used within five days.

- *Evaporated milk* – This is where the amount of liquid has been reduced by evaporation to make a concentrated milk. The milk is reduced to about 50 per cent of its original volume

▲ *A selection of milk products.*

during the process and is homogenized to stop the fat separating out during storage. The milk is then canned, sterilized and cooled.

- *Sweetened condensed milk* — This is milk that has been evaporated and had sugar added to it. Whole, semi-skimmed or skimmed milk can be used.
- *Dried milk* — The moisture is removed from the milk to produce a powder that contains less than five per cent moisture. The milk is homogenized, heat treated and then dried. It will keep in cool, dry conditions for about a year. Once reconstituted (mixed with a liquid) it must be refrigerated and used within five days.
- *Flavoured milks* — These are made from UHT or sterilized milk. They are mostly semi-skimmed or skimmed products.
- *Filled milks* — This is skimmed milk with vegetable fat added. It is available as a dried product as well as liquid.

Functional properties of milk

- The proteins lactalbumin and lactoglobulin **coagulate** on heating, whereas casein does not, unless the milk becomes acid. Milk kept in a warm environment becomes acid very quickly because **bacteria** change the lactose to lactic acid. The increased acid in the milk causes the casein to coagulate. This is referred to as curdling and also occurs when another acid type ingredient, such as lemon juice, is mixed with milk.
- When milk is boiled, casein joins the calcium, the water on the surface of the milk evaporates and a skin is formed on the surface.
- An **enzyme** called rennet is added to some products made with milk to produce a 'set' — most commonly used in cheese-making. When rennet is added the casein coagulates and surrounds the liquid content of the milk to produce the set.

It is said that the **functional properties** of milk are altered when it is homogenized. Scientists have found that sauces and custards made with homogenized milk are more **viscous** and creamy and that the setting qualities are better.

43

resources

Books

Collins Real World Food Technology   Collins
J Inglis & S Plews with E Chapman   1997

Collins Study & Revision Guide: Food Technology GCSE   Collins
J Hotson & J Robinson   1999

Examining Food Technology   Heinemann
Anne Barnett   1996

Food Technology   Collins Educational
Janet Inglis, Sue Plews, Eileen Chapman   1997

GCSE Food Technology for OCR   Heinemann
Jenny Ridgwell   1999

Nuffield D&T: Food technology   Longman
                                                           1996

The Science and Technology of Foods   Forbes Publications
R K Proudlove

Skills in Food Technology   Heinemann
Jenny Ridgwell   1997

Understanding Ingredients   Heinemann Library
Anne Barnett   1998

Contacts

British Nutrition Foundation
High Holborn House
52-54 High Holborn
London WC1V 6RQ
020 7404 6504
www.nutrition.org.uk

*The Food & Drink Industry National
Training Organisation*
6 Catherine Street
London
WC2 5JJ
020 7836 2460
www.foodanddrinknto.org.uk
*More information on training and careers
in food and drink manufacturing.*

Institute of Food Science & Technology
5 Cambridge Court
210 Shepherd's Bush Road
London
W6 7NJ
020 7603 6316
www.ifst.org
*Gives information on food-related
training and careers.*

*Sustain (previously The National Food
Alliance)*
5-11 Worship Street
London
EC2A 2BH
020 7628 7774
*Publications focus on food and its
production, looking at how food is grown,
manufactured, transported and stored.*

I.C.T

www.foodcanmakeyouill.co.uk
A guide to food intolerance.

www.foodforum.org.uk
*Useful for general information about
food, diet and health.*

www.foodtech.org.uk
*A site that is for students as well as
teachers that gives a good overview of
food technology.*

www.quorn.com
*Gives information about its Quorn
products and development.*

glossary

ambient temperature temperature of surroundings, usually room temperature

bacteria a type of micro-organism

baste to pour a liquid, usually fat, over meat before it is roasted

coagulate irreversible process in which proteins 'set' when heat is applied

concentration the amount of a substance, relative to other substances, contained in a mixture or solution. For example, the amount of solute dissolved in a specified amount of solvent or solution.

consistent quality products which are of the same standard whenever they are produced

convection the transfer of heat

conversion the action of changing raw materials into edible products

cross-contamination transfer of bacteria from a contaminated source to an uncontaminated food

duty of care the responsibility of any one involved in food production to ensure that products meet the specification for their development and are of acceptable quality and safe to eat

emboss decorate, cover with a design feature

emulsifier a substance that stabilises an emulsion

emulsion a colloidal system which is a mixture of two substances which normally do not mix without separating

enrobe to coat a food item with something e.g. breadcrumbs on fish fingers

enzyme a substance produced by a living organism which acts as a catalyst (speeder-up of processes) to promote a specific biochemical reaction

extrusion shape a material or mixture by forcing it through a die

fatty acid a substance whose molecules are composed of a long hydrocarbon chain (the 'fatty' bit) and an acid group. A fatty acid combines with glycerol to form fats.

fermentation the chemical breakdown of substances by yeasts, bacteria and other micro-organisms. Used particularly in breadmaking.

foam a mass of small bubbles containing air, produced in food preparation by beating eggs and cake mixtures, for example

formulation a recipe; a list and proportion of ingredients of a mixture

functional property the qualities which a food possesses; the chemical and physical nature of food

fungus (plural fungi) spore producing organism/s, including yeasts, mushrooms, moulds, which feed on organic matter

gluten a 'stretchy' substance produced when the wheat proteins, gliadin and glutenin are mixed with water

hydroxyl combined hydrogen and oxygen

immiscible not able to be mixed

micro-organism a microscopic organism; a bacterium; a fungus

'mouth feel' the sensation experienced in the mouth when food is eaten. The texture of a food material in the mouth.

organoleptic the sensations which food engenders in various organs, such as the nose, the mouth, the eye

pH the measurement of the acidity/alkalinity of a substance

primary product raw materials from which food products are made

secondary product edible food products made from raw materials, for example bread is a secondary product made from flour, yeast and water (and sometimes fat)

sensory attribute the colour, aroma and flavour characteristics of an ingredient or food product

soluble a substance which is capable of dissolving in another substance

solute a substance which dissolves in another to form a solution

solution a mixture of a solvent and a solute, that is a liquid in which another substance is dissolved

solvent a liquid in which another substance dissolves

soya a protein obtained from the beans of a plant; can be used as a replacement for protein from animal sources in certain foods

specification the precise details of a product and/or a process which must be met for successful results

stable (mixture) a mixture which will not separate out into its constituent parts

stearate a saturated fatty acid derived from animals and plants

unit operations the sequenced stages of a process

viscous/vicosity degree of thickness of a substance or a mixture

yeast a microscopic single-celled fungus which can convert sugar into alcohol and carbon dioxide. It reproduces by a budding process. It is used in food production processes, particularly breadmaking.

index